The Best Book of
Polar Animals

Christiane Gunzi

KINGFISHER

NEW YORK

Contents

Created for Kingfisher Publications Plc by Picthall & Gunzi Limited

Author and editor: Christiane Gunzi
Designer: Dominic Zwemmer
Consultant: Theresa Greenaway
Editorial assistance: Lauren Robertson and Barnaby Harward
Illustrators: Michael Langham Rowe, Robin Bouttell, Barry Croucher, Brin Edwards, Rachel Lockwood, Norman Arcott, John Butler, Chris Forsey, John Francis, Alan Harris, Linden Artists Ltd, William Oliver, Bernard Robinson, Denis Ryan, David Wright

KINGFISHER
Larousse Kingfisher Chambers Inc.
80 Maiden Lane
New York, New York 10038
www.kingfisherpub.com

First published in 2002

10 9 8 7 6 5 4 3 2 1

1TR/0102/WKT/MAR(MAR)/128KMA

LIBRARY OF CONGRESS CATALOGING-IN-PUBLICATION DATA has been applied for.

ISBN 0-7534-5435-1

Printed in Hong Kong

Frozen lands

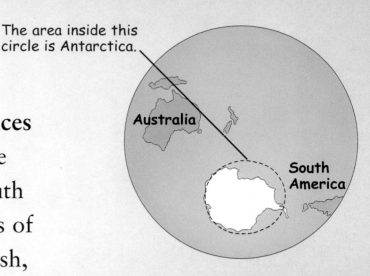

The area inside this circle is Antarctica.

Australia

South America

The polar regions are the wildest, windiest places on Earth. The North Pole is in the Arctic and the South Pole is in Antarctica. These huge areas of snow and ice are bitterly cold and harsh, but many animals can survive there. Some leave during the coldest months of the year and return again in the summer to breed. A few mammals, such as the polar bear and Arctic fox, stay in the Arctic all year round.

Antarctica

This is the coldest place on Earth, with huge icebergs, glaciers, and mountains. In the winter the surrounding sea freezes into thick ice.

Surviving on a sea of ice

In the winter polar bears wander over the frozen Arctic pack ice searching for food. Arctic foxes often follow bears as they hunt for seals under the ice. The fox eats the bear's leftovers. It better not get too close though—in case the bear tries to eat it!

The area inside this circle is the Arctic.

North America

Asia

Europe

Africa

The Arctic

Much of the Arctic is a frozen desert. In the winter the great sea called the Arctic Ocean freezes over, forming a huge blanket of ice.

Musk oxen

Icy winds blow across the Arctic for most of the year. Musk oxen, polar bears, wolves, and foxes can put up with this rough weather because their thick coats keep them warm.

Musk oxen huddle in a circle for warmth and protection

Living in an icy world

The wolf is one of only a few mammals that lives in the Arctic all year round. Thick fur helps protect this predator from the extreme cold. Wolves usually live in packs or in family groups. During the winter they are always on the move, hunting for prey. Arctic wolves can survive for days without eating any food.

Pale fur camouflages Arctic wolves as they hunt for prey around the icy Arctic.

Snowshoe hare

A snowshoe hare has large, furry pads on its feet to help it grip the surface as it runs over the snow and ice. In the winter when the ground is covered with snow, a snowshoe hare's fur turns white. This camouflage helps it hide from predators such as wolves.

Food for the pack

Arctic wolves mainly hunt large prey such as musk oxen and reindeer. They also eat lemmings and hares. One musk ox is enough to feed a wolf pack for several days. Wolves sometimes travel over 600 mi. (1,000km) in search of prey.

Animals of the Arctic

During the coldest months of the year when the ocean freezes over, many animals leave the Arctic. Some spend the winter on the tundra and others migrate farther south until the spring. In the summer the sun shines all day and night in the Arctic, melting the frozen sea ice. Many mammals and birds return at this time to feed and breed during the short Arctic summer.

Spring coat

Summer coat

Winter coat

Arctic fox weighs up to 18 lbs (8kg)

Keeping warm

Foxes, wolves, bears, seals, and musk oxen have thick fur to keep them warm. In the winter their coat is even thicker. The fur of Arctic foxes and hares changes color to camouflage them.

Ringed seal up to 5 ft. (1.5m) long

Harp seal up to 7 ft. (2.2m) long

Beluga up to 18 ft. (5.5m) long

Northern right whale up to 59 ft. (18m) long

8

Snowy owl
up to 25 in.
(65cm) high

Ivory gull
up to 17 in.
(44cm) high

Little auk
up to 8 in.
(20cm) high

Puffin
up to 12 in.
(30cm) high

Ptarmigan
up to 14 in.
(35.5cm) high

Moose
up to 7.5 ft.
(2.3m) high

Musk ox
up to 5 ft.
(1.5m) high

Polar bear
up to 5.3 ft.
(1.6m) high

Walrus
up to 12 ft.
(3.7m) long

Narwhal
up to 15.5 ft.
(4.7m) long

Animals of the Antarctic

The only mammals that live in the Antarctic are whales and seals.
There are many kinds of seabirds, and the water is filled with fish.

In the winter the sea surrounding Antarctica freezes over, and the continent almost doubles in size. Many animals migrate to warmer areas and return in the summer.
The emperor penguin is one of the few animals that lives in Antarctica all year round.

Elephant seal up to 20 ft. (6m) long

Ross seal up to 10 ft. (3m) long

Leopard seal up to 12 ft. (3.6m) long

Fin whale up to 85 ft. (26m) long

Humpback whale up to 52.5 ft (16m) long

Marble plunderfish up to 12 in. (30cm) long

Adélie penguin
up to 28 in.
(71cm)
high

Black-browed
albatross
wingspan up
to 8 ft. (2.4m)

Brown skua
up to 23 in.
(58cm) high

Body warmers

Seals and whales have blubber
under their skin to protect them
in the icy water. Seabirds such
as penguins also have fat under
their skin and layers of down
and feathers to keep out the cold.

Sheathbill
up to 17 in.
(43cm) high

Emperor penguin
up to 3.6 ft.
(1.1m) high

Weddell seal
up to 8.5 ft.
(2.6m) long

Ice fish
up to 30 in.
(75cm) long

The tundra in the summer

Around the Arctic there is a huge frozen plain called the tundra where no trees grow. In the winter it is dark for most of the time, and the temperature falls far below zero. In the summer the ice melts, and the tundra bursts into life with colorful flowers and insects. Grass, moss, and lichen provide food for musk oxen and other plant eaters.

Snowy owl

Hunters on the tundra

The snowy owl hunts during the day for lemmings, voles, and hares. It sometimes catches other birds too. Lynxes, wolves, and foxes also hunt on the tundra.

Lynx

Cottongrass

Lichen

Arctic poppy

Ptarmigan

12

Reindeer

Many mammals, such as lemmings, live on the tundra all year round. Reindeer spend the winter in forests 600 mi. (1,000km) farther south. In the summer reindeer return to the tundra in herds to breed and feed on the thick grass.

Reindeer with calf

Dragonfly

Musk oxen

Purple saxifrage

Moss campion

Fritillary butterfly

Lemmings

13

The great sea bear

The polar bear is king of the Arctic. This mammal is an excellent swimmer, and its toes are partially webbed to help it paddle along in the water. The polar bear's pale, thick fur keeps it warm during the Arctic winter. Each hair is hollow, so the fur is not heavy when it gets wet. The bear can swim for long distances without stopping.

Sneaking up on seals

A polar bear's favorite prey is seals. It can smell a seal from almost a mile away, and it sometimes follows them for hundreds of miles. The polar bear usually sneaks up on the seals from behind. If they see a bear approaching, seals dive into the water and swim away.

Ringed seals on
the lookout for
polar bears

A polar bear swims with just
its head poking out of the water

15

Snow babies

Male polar bears often spend the winter hunting on the sea ice. But the female settles into a winter den on the side of a hill, far away from other bears. After about 60 days one or two fluffy, white cubs are born. The newborn cubs are tiny, but they grow fast because their mother's milk is very nutritious. The cubs usually stay with their mother for the first two years.

1 At first the tiny, newborn cubs are blind and helpless. They start to feed on their mother's milk right away and she washes them.

2 The mother bear does not eat all winter while she is taking care of her cubs. She becomes very thin, but her cubs grow strong.

3 In the spring the female leads her cubs out of the den. She is very hungry and has to hunt for food. The cubs will watch their mother hunt and begin to copy her.

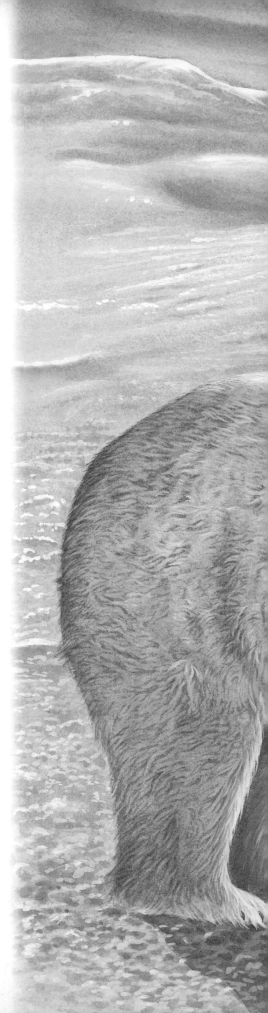

Caring for cubs

A female bear never lets her cubs stray far from her. She guards them carefully in case a large male tries to kill them. The male polar bear is much heavier than the female—and stronger too.

Female polar bear guarding her young cubs against a male

Polar fox

The Arctic fox is well equipped for its frozen home. It has furry pads on each foot so it can run long distances on the cold snow and ice, hunting for food. Thick, fine fur keeps the fox warm—and at the coldest times of the year the fox digs tunnels under the snow for shelter. Other animals find it difficult to see the fox as it races across the snow in its white winter coat.

Ringed seal pup

Arctic hare

Ptarmigan

Shore crab

Barnacle goose eggs

Berries

Vole

Changing color

The fox's coat camouflages it in the summer and the winter as it hunts for prey. In the summer its coat is grayish-brown. This turns into a white coat for the icy winter.

Ground squirrel

Food for Arctic foxes

In the summer there is plenty of food for foxes, including ground squirrels, voles, birds, and berries. Foxes bury a supply of food in the summer and save it for the winter.

18

Living on leftovers

Foxes are scavengers. In the winter when there is not much to eat, they depend on polar bears to catch their food. The fox eats the bear's leftovers. Later, gulls come along and eat what the fox has left. Nothing is wasted.

Polar bear wandering off after feeding on a seal

19

Ice fish

Antarctic krill

Antarctic cod

Sea spider

Isopod

Antarctic krill

This shrimplike crustacean is the main
food of whales that visit the Antarctic
Ocean to feed. There can be millions
of krill in one group. Krill feed on
algae growing beneath the ice.

Deep beneath the ice

There are at least 200 kinds of fish living under the frozen sea ice of the Antarctic, but scientists know little about how they live. Most of these fish are types of cod and ice fish. They have a special substance in their blood that stops their body from freezing. As well as fish, many other kinds of animals are found in the seas around Antarctica, including squid, starfish, jellyfish, krill, seals, and huge whales.

Jellyfish

Squid

Starfish

Migrating minke

The minke whale migrates to the Antarctic in the summer to feed on the huge swarms of krill in the sea. This small baleen whale is one of the most common whales in the Antarctic.

21

Super swimmers

Walruses and seals have a thick layer of fat, or blubber, to keep them warm. These sea mammals spend much of their lives in the water and swim using their flippers. Some can dive to great depths to find food and hold their breath underwater for up to half an hour each time. Seals hunt for fish, mollusks, and crustaceans. Walruses use their long tusks to dig around on the seabed, searching for clams and other mollusks.

Wandering walruses

Walruses live near the edge of the Arctic ice all year. In the summer they swim farther north to breed. Walruses are huge and heavy, but they are very good swimmers.

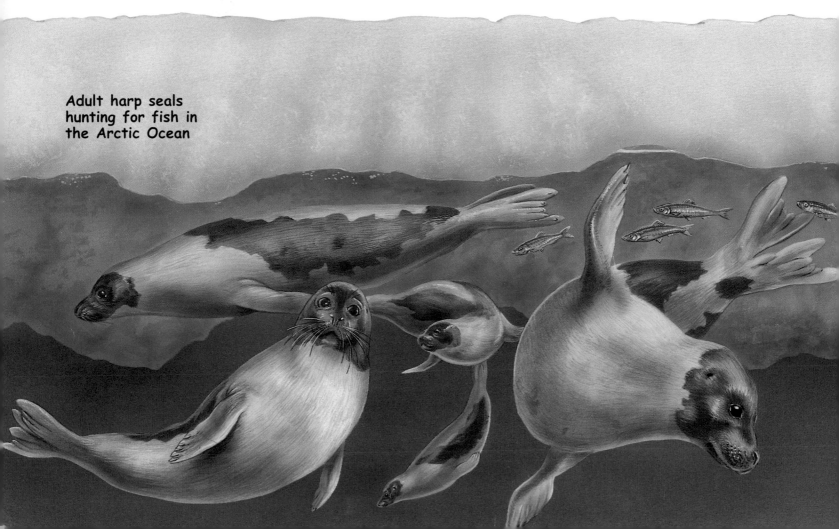

Adult harp seals hunting for fish in the Arctic Ocean

Leopard of the sea

The leopard seal is the fiercest predator in the Antarctic. It patrols the edge of the sea ice waiting for penguins to dive into the water. Leopard seals also feed on krill, and they sometimes hunt other seals.

Leopard seal chasing an Adélie penguin

Harp seal pup on the ice

Harp seal

A harp seal pup feeds on its mother's milk for just 12 days. Then the female leaves it on its own. The pup's pale fur helps camouflage it.

Flying in the waves

Penguins are perfectly equipped for life in the water. These birds are clumsy on land, but in the ocean they are agile and graceful. A penguin's body is smooth and streamlined like a seal's, so it can glide through the waves with ease. Tough feathers and a thick layer of fat keep Antarctic penguins warm. Some of them live in huge groups called colonies.

Types of penguins

There are 17 types of penguins. Emperor, king, gentoo, rockhopper, chinstrap, and Adélie penguins live in Antarctica. The macaroni penguin lives on islands that are close to Antarctica.

Emperor's new clothes

An emperor penguin chick is covered in fluffy down to protect it from cold winds. To keep warm, the chick stands on its parent's feet!

Emperor
up to 47 in.
(120cm)

King
up to 36 in.
(90cm)

Macaroni
up to 30 in.
(76cm)

Chinstrap
up to 29 in.
(75cm)

Gentoo
up to 29 in.
(75cm)

Rockhopper
up to 25 in.
(63cm)

Adélie penguins
walking to the sea
from their rookery

Taking a dip

Penguins are excellent swimmers and
divers, and they seem to fly through the
water. They stay under for a few minutes
and then come up to the surface to breathe.
Adélie penguins sometimes swim over 60 miles
(100km) from the shore to feed on krill.

Penguins paddle with
their "wings" and steer
with their tails

All kinds of seabirds

Huge numbers of birds visit the polar regions, including gulls, terns, albatrosses, and petrels. Most of these seabirds make nests on islands where they gather in large colonies. A few birds, such as emperor and Adélie penguins, actually breed on the continent of Antarctica. Seabirds feed on fish, squid, octopuses, and crustaceans. They glide above the ocean, then dive into the waves to grab their prey.

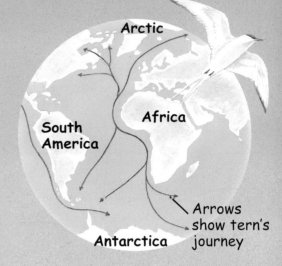

Arctic

South America

Africa

Antarctica

Arrows show tern's journey

Travels of the tern

Arctic terns breed in the Arctic in the summer. When the winter arrives, they fly to Antarctica.

Blue-eyed shag

Gray-winged petrel

Arctic tern

South Georgia pipit

Wandering albatross

This huge seabird roams over the oceans, searching for octopuses, cuttlefish, and squid. Its enormous wings span about 10 ft. (3m) from tip to tip.

Wandering albatross

Wilson's storm petrel

Ivory gull

Brown skua

27

Polar life in danger

People mine for coal and oil in the Arctic, which damages the wildlife there. Now many countries have agreed not to mine or drill for minerals in Antarctica for at least 40 years. This important agreement is called the Antarctic Treaty. If people start mining or drilling for oil in Antarctica, the animals there will be harmed. Antarctica is the only wild place on Earth that is not being damaged by humans. It is important not to pollute it.

Poisoned polar bears

The Arctic is being polluted by human garbage. Polar bears, foxes, and other animals wander over garbage dumps that people use, searching for food. As the animals eat the scraps that they find they are often injured by broken containers. The animals are also poisoned when they swallow harmful liquids such as chemicals.

Polar bear searching for scraps of food at a garbage dump

An animal rescuer
cleaning oil off
of the beach

Oil spills in the ocean

Huge ships that carry oil
sometimes sink, leaking the
oil into the oceans. Slicks
form on the water and over
beaches. When polar animals
become covered in sticky
oil, they are not able to
move around or breathe
correctly. They usually die
if the oil is not removed.

29

Saving polar life

We must protect the Arctic and Antarctic so that animals living there, such as polar bears, seals, penguins, and whales, can survive into the future. Many people believe that the polar areas should be turned into huge nature reserves. This would mean that all polar animals would be able to live in their natural habitats without being disturbed by people.

Saving baby seals

To stop people from killing seal pups for their beautiful, white fur, a bright red dye is sprayed over their coats. The dye does not harm the pups and fades after a while.

Chinstrap penguins being filmed in their Antarctic nesting site

Studying wildlife

Experts study animals in their natural habitats to find out how they live and how to protect them in the wild.

Television crews film polar wildlife so that people can learn about animals without having to travel to the Poles.

Glossary

algae Simple plants, including seaweed and phytoplankton.

Antarctic The south polar region. This includes the continent of Antarctica and its oceans.

Arctic The ice-covered region around the North Pole.

baleen The huge, fringed plates inside the mouths of baleen whales such as the minke whale.

blubber The thick layer of fat beneath the skin of a whale, seal, or walrus that keeps it warm.

calf A baby whale, deer, cow, dolphin, or elephant.

camouflage The colors, patterns, and markings on an animal that help it hide in the wilderness.

carnivores Animals such as seals, polar bears, and wolves that kill and eat other animals.

crustaceans Certain animals, such as krill, shrimp, lobsters, and crabs, that have a hard outer covering. Most kinds of crustaceans live in the oceans.

glacier A river of ice that moves very slowly.

habitat An animal's habitat is its natural home. A penguin's habitat is the frozen land and cold seas of the Antarctic.

herd A large group of mammals such as reindeer or cattle that live together.

iceberg A huge lump of ice that has broken off from a glacier or an ice shelf. Only a tiny part of the iceberg shows above the surface of the sea.

krill Shrimplike crustaceans that live in the oceans in huge groups called swarms.

mammals Animals such as wolves that are covered in fur or hair, give birth to live young instead of laying eggs, and feed their young milk.

migrate Animals migrate when they travel from one area to another to find food or to breed.

plankton Tiny creatures and plants that live in the sea.

predator An animal that hunts other animals.

prey Any creature that is killed and eaten by another animal.

rookery The home for a group of penguins, walruses, or seals.

scavenger An animal such as an Arctic fox that feeds on food left by other animals.

territory The area where an animal lives.

tundra The area of treeless land between the most northern forests in the world and the ice surrounding the North Pole.

tusk An animal's tooth that grows very long.

31

Index